ROCKY MOUNTAIN
MAJESTY

ALBERTA COLOR

About this book

This impressive collection contains over 100 superb photographs featuring the unique beauty and grand diversity of the Canadian Rockies. A memorable souvenir, a treasured gift or an interesting reference, "Rocky Mountain Majesty" is a showcase for the scenic beauty of this spectacular area of Canada.

Other titles from Alberta Color

Alberta Beauty, A Portrait of the Province
Picture Perfect Edmonton
Jasper Treasures, Beauty in the Canadian Rockies
The Canadian Rockies, Land of the Shining Mountains
Canada's Rocky Mountains

Front Cover
Moraine Lake, Banff National Park

Design, Editorial & Photography
Ron & Noreen Kelly, Alberta Color
Additional Photography by J. Sutton & S. Hong

Revisit the beauty of Canada at our website www.beautyseen.com

Published & Distributed by
Alberta Color
4149 98 Street
Edmonton, Alberta
Canada T6E 5N5

MADE IN CANADA

At A Glance

Mountains

The Canadian Rockies are famous the world over for their spectacular scenery and pristine wilderness.

The "Shining Mountains," as they were known to early aboriginal peoples, comprise a mountainous region in Western Canada of 180,000 sq. km (69,500 sq. mi.). They cover a large area of western Alberta and eastern British Columbia.

The geology of these mountains is primarily sedimentary rock up to 1.5 billion years old. Over a period of 100 million years, the collision of the Earth's plates caused sediments on the sea bottom of the west-coast continental shelf to be fractured and thrust upward. These sheets of folded and broken rock form the awe-inspiring peaks of today.

The highest mountain in the Canadian Rockies is lofty Mount Robson, pictured here. "The Emperor" of the Rockies is located just west of Jasper National Park. It reaches an impressive height of 3,954 m (12,972 ft.), but there are many peaks in the Rockies that stand above 3,500 m (11,480 ft.).

Over a hundred years ago, some forward-thinking Canadians were inspired to conserve these ranges in a series of national and provincial parks. Today, the parks play a vital role as living nature sanctuaries, for all to experience and treasure.

The shape of Mount Rundle, near the Banff townsite, displays the classic lines of an "overthrust" mountain, resulting from sheets of rock sliding up and over each other during mountain building.

A colourful sunrise paints Rundle's distinctive slopes and their reflection in the calm water of the Vermilion Lakes, *right*. Sulphur Mountain, the location of Banff's famous Hot Springs, stands beside in silhouette.

Moose Cow & Calf

Northwest Face of Mount Rundle

Mount Rundle & Sulphur Mountain, Banff National Park

The rugged snow-capped beauty of Mount Edith Cavell, one of the highest peaks in the Jasper area, rises above the shimmering water of Cavell Lake.

Grizzly Bear

Castle Mountain, Banff National Park

The steep walls and turrets of Castle Mountain, *left,* are trademarks of the "castellated" peaks commonly seen in the Rockies.

Castle Mountain overlooks the Bow River, halfway between Banff and Lake Louise. Prospecting for minerals once revealed promising deposits of copper and lead in the mountain, but these were never developed. Such exploration is now prohibited.

Mount Columbia, *left,* the highest mountain in Alberta, is a typical "horn" mountain, its triangular shape the result of simultaneous glaciation on different sides of the peak.

The Ramparts, *right,* located in Jasper and straddling the Continental Divide between Alberta and British Columbia, form one of the great mountain walls of the Canadian Rockies.

Bobcat

The Ramparts, Jasper National Park

Cascade Mountain, Banff National Park

Cascade Mountain is a familiar landmark in Banff, where it provides a stunning backdrop behind Banff Avenue, *left*. The summer view of the mountain is edged with the beautiful flower beds and gardens of the Banff Park Administration Centre, *right*.

Mule Deer

Mount Assiniboine, Mount Assiniboine Provincial Park

Mount Temple, Banff National Park

Mighty Mount Temple, *right*, is the highest peak in the Lake Louise area, with an elevation of 3,544 m (11,627 ft.).

The steep summit of Mount Assiniboine, *left*, towers above surrounding peaks southwest of Banff. This impressive mountain is accessible only on foot or by helicopter.

Shrubby Potentilla

The Three Sisters, Canmore

A trio of peaks known as The Three Sisters, *left*, is the signature landmark of Canmore, a thriving mountain community east of Banff.

The magnificent Continental Range, *right*, on the eastern edge of the Rockies, is part of David Thompson Country. This pristine protected area is named for an early explorer.

Cougar

Peaks in the Continental Range, David Thompson Country

Lakes

Impossibly vivid lakes, the precious jewels of the Canadian Rockies, add splashes of spectacular and unexpected colour to the rugged landscape.

Most lakes in the Rockies are fed by meltwater from glaciers. When the stream of glacial water slows as it enters the lake, larger particles of gravel, rock, sand and dust gradually fall out. These deposits often build a delta out from the shore. Finely ground glacial sediment, or rock flour, remains suspended in the water. The minute and uniform size of these sediment particles allows them to reflect the blue and green wavelengths of light, and gives the mountain lakes their unforgettable hues.

Many mountain lakes are naturally dammed by moraines, landforms created from the rubble, or till, resulting from glaciation.

The calm and brilliant water of Moraine Lake, *right,* reflects the massive mountain wall behind the lake. This is the Valley of the Ten Peaks, "The Wenkchemna Peaks," a view featured on the Canadian twenty-dollar bill until 1989.

Clark's Nutcracker

Lake Louise, Banff National Park

A world-famous icon of the Canadian Rockies, lovely Lake Louise, *left*, is fed by glaciers at the foot of Mount Victoria, 10 km (6 mi.) across the lake. The tranquil blue-green water is especially calm in the morning.

Deer Fawn

Lake Louise, Banff National Park

Lake Louise, Banff National Park

Moose Calf

The crystal water of Maligne Lake enhances the view of Samson Peak, *above*, a striking peak named for Stoney Indian chief Samson Beaver.

The largest natural body of water in the Canadian Rockies, Maligne Lake is also the location of beautiful Spirit Island, *right*, a small promontory of land that extends into the lake near Samson Narrows. Cruiseboat tours allow this famous scene to be enjoyed by many visitors every year.

Maligne Lake, Jasper National Park

In winter, the 23 km (14 mi.) length of Maligne Lake is a frozen panorama of ice and snow. The familiar peaks of Mount Charlton and Mount Unwin stand on the right.

The historic boathouse at Maligne Lake, *left*, was originally built by guide and outfitter Curly Phillips in 1929 and is still in use today.

Ground Squirrel

Waterton Lakes National Park, "where the mountains meet the prairie," is an area of unique beauty in the southwest corner of Alberta.

Upper Waterton Lake is the deepest lake in the Canadian Rockies with a maximum depth of 157 m (515 ft.). Appropriately, the name Waterton is from the Blackfoot Indian words for "big water." The southern end of the lake crosses into Glacier National Park in Montana, U.S.A.

Mule Deer

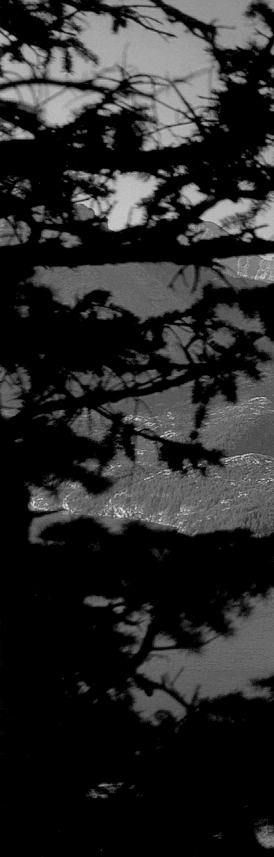

Pink fireweed skirts the edge of Bow Lake, *left*, one of many gorgeous lakes along the Icefield Parkway.

Surrounded by snow-clad peaks, Bow Lake, *right*, lies under an icy winter blanket. However, the glaciers that feed the lake melt year-round; the water flowing under the ice is the source of the Bow River.

Black Bear Cub

Bow Lake, Banff National Park

Medicine Lake, Jasper National Park

Due to a unique natural underground drainage system, water levels in Medicine Lake, *left*, vary dramatically thoughout the year.

Spring run-off sometimes brings flooding as the lake levels rise. But by fall, the water almost disappears and all that remains is a braided stream flowing over the partially exposed lake bottom.

Grey Wolf

Appropriately named Emerald Lake, *right*, is the largest of many beautiful lakes located in Yoho National Park in British Columbia.

Surrounded by high mountains, Emerald Lake receives abundant year-round precipitation, allowing the area to support a rich variety of vegetation.

Bull & Cow Elk

Emerald Lake, Yoho National Park

Peyto Lake, Banff National Park

The Bow Summit Viewpoint rewards travellers on the Icefield Parkway with a fine panorama of Peyto Lake, Mount Patterson and the Mistaya Valley, *left*.

Named for Bill Peyto, an eccentric character from the early days of mountain guiding, Peyto Lake is the fifth-largest lake in Banff National Park.

Rocky Mountain Bighorn Sheep

Glaciers & Rivers

The massive icefields of the Canadian Rockies are remnants of the huge sheets of ice that covered the area during ancient ice ages.

Glaciers are the main eroding force in the mountains, slowly grinding the rock into fragments of rock flour, widening and deepening valleys, nestling into bowl-shaped cirques and hanging from steep summits.

Glaciers in the Rockies are frozen rivers of ice, but they are also the source of fresh water for much of the extensive river system in Canada. Meltwaters from the Columbia Icefield flow to the Pacific, the Atlantic and the Arctic Oceans. The summit of Snow Dome, *right*, is the apex of this tri-oceanic watershed.

The Canadian Rockies encompass over sixteen icefields and countless glaciers. The Clemenceau Icefield & Tusk Peak, *left*, reveal an awesome glimpse of pristine beauty in a vast sea of ice.

The Columbia Icefield covers 300 sq. km (115 sq. mi.) and is the largest accumulation of ice in the Rockies. It is also the most accessible; several of its spectacular glaciers are easily visible from the Icefield Parkway.

The Athabasca Glacier, *right,* descends in a series of three icefalls from the main icefield. Specially designed snocoaches, *below,* allow visitors close-up views of the glacier.

Athabasca Glacier at the Columbia Icefield, Jasper National Park

Athabasca Glacier, Jasper National Park

A huge backdrop of ice dwarfs hikers at the base of the Athabasca Glacier, *left*.

The surface of the glacier is patterned with deep crevasses, fissures which form when the brittle upper layers of ice crack and split. There may be over 30,000 crevasses on the Athabasca Glacier.

Glacial Crevasse

Saskatchewan Glacier, Banff National Park

The Saskatchewan Glacier, *left,* descends from the eastern edge of the Columbia Icefield into Banff National Park. Meltwater from this glacier feeds the North Saskatchewan River system and eventually flows into Hudson's Bay.

Mount Kitchener, a glacier-clad peak at the northern end of the Columbia Icefield, is reflected in Beauty Creek, *right,* an aptly named stop along the Icefield Parkway.

Grizzly Bear Cubs

Bow River & Castle Mountain, Banff National Park

The Bow River, *left*, the longest river in Banff National Park, flows by the foot of Castle Mountain and winds its way along the valley floor, heading towards the flat land of southern Alberta.

Bull Elk, or Wapiti, a native Shawnee word meaning "white rump"

Maligne River, Jasper National Park

Winter's cold slows the Maligne River, *left*, and tames the many rapids that roll in this swift river during the summer.

The Kicking Horse River, *right*, has carved a narrow channel through the erosion-resistant sedimentary rock that forms The Natural Bridge in Yoho National Park.

Mountain Goat

Kicking Horse River, Yoho National Park

Athabasca River, Jasper National Park

The Athabasca River, *right*, is a typical glacier-fed river of the Canadian Rockies, characterized by many braided streams. This Canadian Heritage river drains more than half of Jasper National Park.

The distinctive snowy peak of Mount Edith Cavell graces the far horizon.

North Saskatchewan River, Banff National Park

Sunwapta River, Jasper National Park

The spectacular Icefield Parkway follows the valley of the Sunwapta River, *right*, as it flows north from the lake at the toe of the Athabasca Glacier.

The glacier-fed North Saskatchewan River, *left*, is over 1,200 km (750 mi.) long, and gathers the water of many streams and tributaries as it heads towards the prairies. Saskatchewan is a Cree word meaning "swift water."

Cougar Cub

Canyons & Falls

The steep canyons and thundering waterfalls of the Canadian Rockies are truly awe-inspiring.

The canyons are spectacular, narrow-walled gorges eroded by fast-flowing streams and rivers. The crashing force of the water, along with the effect of naturally acidic rainwater and the grinding action of coarse glacial silt, wears away the limestone bedrock.

Tumbling over ledges and rushing through gorges, the waterfalls of the mountains create fantastic scenes. Some falls, such as Takakkaw, cascade from "hanging valleys," spilling into an eroded channel from high above.

Many waterfalls are unnamed and seasonal, like the one to the left, hurrying to add its water to one of the many beautiful mountain lakes.

Exquisite Agnes Falls, *right*, is a wonderful highlight of the hike above Lake Louise to Mirror Lake and Lake Agnes.

Sunwapta Falls, Jasper National Park

Tangle Falls, Jasper National Park

Tangle Creek splashes over a series of rocky ledges beside the Icefield Parkway to create picturesque Tangle Falls, *right*,

Ice cold and full of silt from the Athabasca Glacier, the Sunwapta River splits its path around a small island of trees before tumbling over Sunwapta Falls, *left*.

Timber Wolf Pups

Takakkaw Falls, Yoho National Park

The best-known waterfall in Yoho National Park is Takakkaw Falls, a lofty cascade fed by the meltwaters of the Daly Glacier in British Columbia.

The booming thunder of these tremendous falls can be heard from a considerable distance. One of the highest waterfalls in Canada, Takakkaw is arguably the most impressive falls in the Rockies, especially at peak flow.

Great Horned Owl

Athabasca Falls, Jasper National Park

The Athabasca River carries the most water of any river in the Rocky Mountain Parks. When it thunders over the Athabasca Falls, *left,* the sights and sounds are incredible. Spray from the falls keeps the area moist and sustains a canyon forest of pine, fir and spruce.

Broad-shouldered Mount Kerkeslin, a familiar landmark along the Icefield Parkway south of Jasper townsite, rises behind the falls, *right.*

Black Bear

Cameron Falls, Waterton Lakes National Park

Cameron Falls, *left*, becomes a fabulous ice sculpture in winter, a frozen mass of gigantic icicles. The limestone here in Waterton Lakes Park is over 1.5 billion years old, some of the oldest visible rock in the Canadian Rockies.

Grizzly Bear

An ingenious system of suspended walkways allows close-up access to the limestone walls of Johnston Canyon, *right*, located west of the Banff townsite. Several lovely waterfalls are created by Johnston Creek as it rushes through the canyon.

Mountain Goat Kid

Johnston Canyon, Banff National Park

Maligne Canyon, Jasper National Park

With a maximum depth of 55 m (180 ft.) Maligne Canyon, *left,* is the deepest limestone canyon in the Rockies. Airborne spray from the rushing water of the Maligne River coats the steep canyon walls and supports moisture-loving plants.

Rocky Mountain Bighorn Sheep

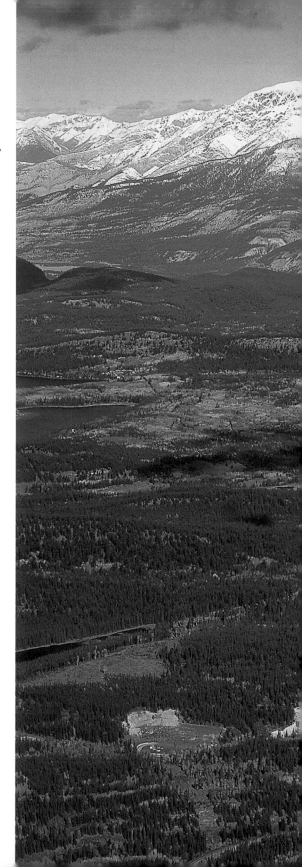

Towns

The first human inhabitants of the Canadian Rockies were various tribes of aboriginal peoples. Many present day place-names originate in native tongues.

The building of the Canadian Pacific Railway, completed in 1885, provided a great impetus for European settlement in the mountains. Banff and Jasper Parks were formed in part to preserve areas of wilderness from advancing development.

The mountain towns of today are thriving tourist destinations, and are under continued pressure to maintain the wilderness mandate of the parks. Surrounded by great beauty, they are trusted to be diligent stewards of the pristine splendour of the Canadian Rockies.

The scenic town of Jasper, *right*, nestles in the valleys of the Miette and Athabasca Rivers, surrounded by pretty mountain lakes. Visitors can gain a panoramic view of the townsite by riding the Jasper Tramway, *left*, to the top of nearby Whistlers Mountain.

Banff Townsite & Mount Rundle, Banff National Park

Banff was Canada's first National Park, created in 1885 after the discovery of mineral hot springs on Sulphur Mountain caused a great stir of interest in the area. The townsite is situated in the Bow River Valley and is distinguished by the familiar peaks of Mount Rundle, *far left*, and Cascade and Tunnel Mountains, *below*.

Common Fireweed

Banff Springs Hotel, Banff National Park

Banff Springs Hotel, the famous "castle in the mountains," overlooks the Bow River and Bow Falls. The hotel offers luxury accommodation in a legendary mountain setting. This view has become one of the icons of the Canadian Rockies.

Grey Wolf

Prince of Wales Hotel, Waterton National Park

The Great Northern Railway constructed the Prince of Wales Hotel, *left*, in 1926 to provide an overnight stop for bus tours from Glacier Park in the United States. Today, the hotel offers visitors to Waterton Lakes National Park unique accommodation with a grand mountain view.

Plains Bison

Jasper Park Lodge, Jasper National Park

The Athabasca River provides a beautiful backdrop for Jasper Park Lodge. The lodge is surrounded by vivid mountain lakes and a world-class golf course.

Built in the early 1920s, the main lodge in the original hotel burned to the ground in 1952, but was soon rebuilt in its present sumptuous style.

Mallard Duck